W9-AHS-095

WORLD OF ANIMALS

BUGS

BROWN BEAR BOOKS

Published by Brown Bear Books Limited

An imprint of
The Brown Reference Group plc
68 Topstone Road
Redding
Connecticut
06896
USA
www.brownreference.com

© 2008 The Brown Reference Group plc

This hardcover edition is distributed in the
United States by
Black Rabbit Books
P.O. Box 3263
Mankato, MN 56002

Library of Congress Cataloging-in-Publication Data
Hardyman, Robyn.
  Bugs / by Robyn Hardyman.
    p. cm. -- (The world of animals)
  Includes index.
  Summary: "Describes the behavior, physical
      characteristics, and habitats of common
      insects and spiders"--Provided by publisher.
  ISBN-13: 978-1-933834-36-8
1. Insects--Juvenile literature. I. Title.
QL467.2.H38 2009
595.7--dc22
                    2007049948

ISBN-13: 978-1-933834-36-8
ISBN-10: 1-933834-36-6

For the Brown Reference Group plc
Designer: Paul Myerscough
Editor: Sarah Eason
Creative Director: Jeni Child
Children's Publisher: Anne O'Daly
Editorial Director: Lindsey Lowe

Consultant
Darrin Lunde, Collections Manager, Department of
    Mammalogy, American Museum of Natural
    History, New York, NY

Printed in the United States

Photographic credits:
Front Cover: Nature PL: Arco
Nature PL: Kerstin Hinze 12, Meul/Arco 20,
Premaphotos 13t, Kim Taylor 29b; **NHPA:** N. A.
Callow 21t; **Photolibrary.com:** Anthony Bannister
24, David M. Dennis 6, Juniors Bildarchiv 15b,
Manfred P. Kage 1, 26, Dennis Kunkel 7t, 9, Satoshi
Kuribayashi 23, London Scientific Films 18, Bryan
Reynolds 17tl; **Photos.com:** 25t; **Shutterstock:**
Andrey Armyagov 5, Alan Robert Jupp 15t, Carthy
Keifer 16, 28, 31, Alexander M. Omelko 10, Mark
William Penny 4, Tomasz Pietryszek 21b.

Contents

Any words that appear in the text in bold, **like this**, are explained in the glossary.

What Is a Bug?

There are more bugs than any other animal in the world! Bugs are all around us. Some fly, some swim, some creep and crawl on the land.

Bugs are **insects**. All insects have six legs and a body split into three parts, or sections. Spiders are also called bugs, although they are not insects. Spiders have eight legs and only two parts to their body. Some bugs eat plants and some feed on other insects. They all belong to a group of animals called **invertebrates**. These are animals without a backbone.

Ants are insects. Like many insects, they live in large groups.

Bug World

Scientists have named about a million different kinds of insect so far. There may be millions more still to be named!

Centipede

Dragonfly

Here are just a few of the many insects that live in our world.

Cricket

Louse

Wasp

Butterfly

Antenna

Head

Leg

Thorax (midbody)

Abdomen (rear)

Beetles

UP CLOSE

Insects have three sections to their body, called the head, **thorax**, and **abdomen**. They also have six legs, which are attached to the thorax. Insects feel and smell things with their feelers, called jointed **antennae**.

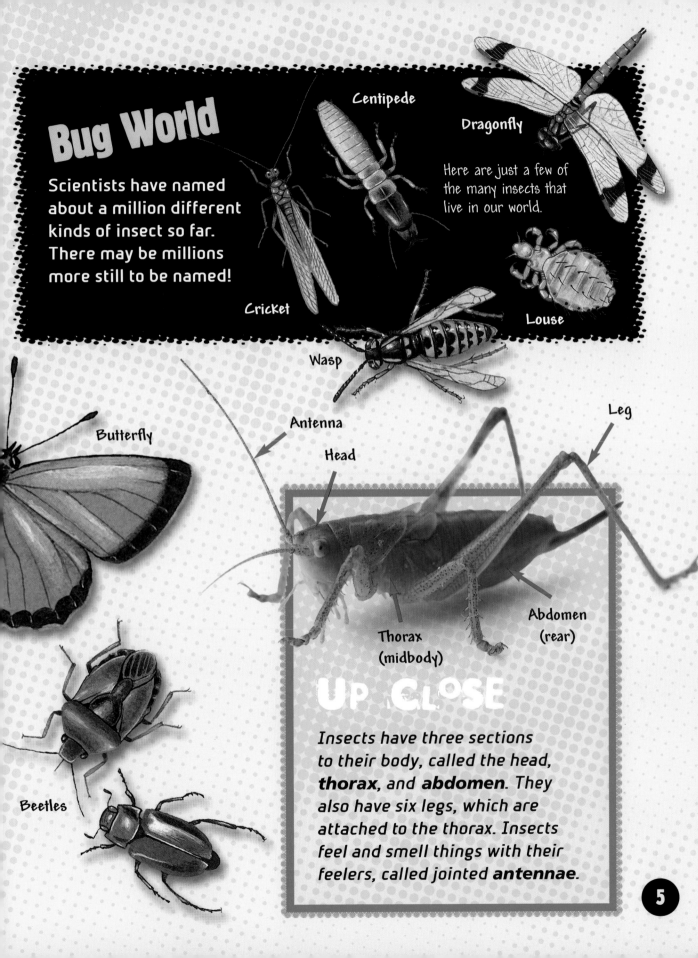

Bedbug

These tiny bugs could be in your bedroom! You might not be able to see them, but at night they come out from their hiding places and feed on blood.

Bedbugs live in houses. By day they hide in cracks and holes in the walls and furniture, at night they hunt for food. Bedbugs have a flat body that helps them squeeze into small spaces. Some bedbugs feed on chickens and other animals. Two kinds of bedbugs feed on humans. Their bites itch but are not dangerous.

This bedbug's body is swollen with blood.

Bloodsucker

A bedbug crawls over its victim and bites them every few steps. It uses a **rostrum** (pink, in photo) on the tip of its head to suck up the blood. The rostrum is a sucking mouthpart with a sharp end that can pierce skin.

Bedbugs do not need to feed very often. They can survive for more than a year without a meal.

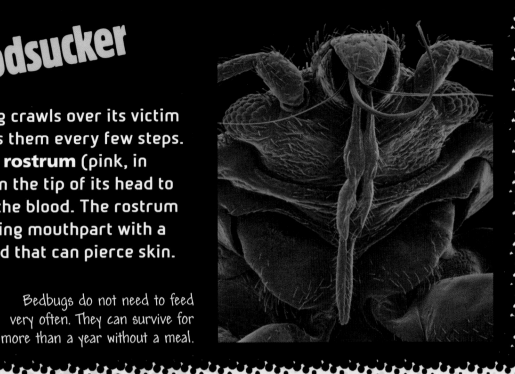

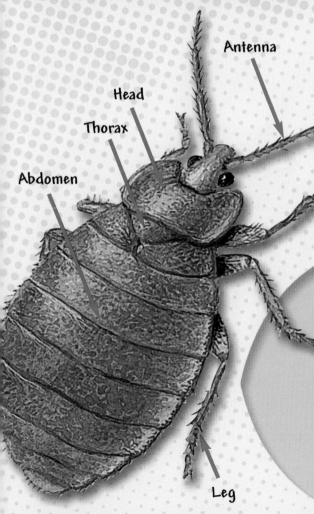

Antenna

Head

Thorax

Abdomen

Leg

UP CLOSE

Female bedbugs lay their eggs in their daytime hiding places. Bedbugs can lay 150–345 eggs in their lifetime. These **insects** live for up to 18 months.

FACT FILE

Common name: bedbug
Scientific name: Cimicidae
Length: from about 0.1 in (3 mm) to 0.2 in (5 mm)
Key features: oval, flattened body, yellow-brown body, no wings
Diet: blood

Head Louse

These bugs really get in your hair! Head lice live only on people—they love to suck blood from your head! Head lice also lay their eggs in people's hair.

Head lice are **parasites**. This means they live on other animals, called **hosts**, and use them for food. Lice cannot fly or jump. They cling to hairs with their claws and attach their eggs to the hairs. The young head lice hatch and feed on the host's blood. Head lice breathe through holes on the sides of their body. They can close these holes when people shampoo their hair, so the lice do not drown.

Head

Thorax

Hair

Leg

Abdomen

FACT FILE

Common name: head louse
Scientific name: *Pediculus humanus*
Length: from about 0.02 in (0.5 mm) to 0.4 in (10 mm)
Key features: flattened body, no wings, short **antennae**, and sucking mouthpart
Diet: human blood

Head lice are small **insects**. They are about the size of a sesame seed. Their bodies are light brown, but turn red after a meal of blood!

Human Parasites

Human head lice carry and pass on more diseases than most other bugs. These diseases include typhus fever and trench fever, which can kill people.

A head louse's strong, curved claws help it grip onto its victim's hair while it sucks blood.

Stag Beetle

The huge, branching jaws of this bug look like the antlers of a **stag**. That is why it is called a stag beetle. Male stag beetles use their giant jaws to fight each other.

Stag beetles come in many colors, from reddish brown to blue, green, violet, or bronze. You can always identify them by their huge jaws and long legs. They live in woodlands and in parts of cities where there are old trees. They sit on the trees during the day. Stag beetles are active mainly at night. The males fly about looking for females.

A male stag beetle sits on a tree and displays its jaws.

Drunk Beetles!

Stag beetles are attracted to a **sap** that runs down damaged trees. The sap can contain alcohol. When the beetles eat it they become drunk, lose their grip, and fall to the ground!

FACT FILE

Common name: stag beetle
Scientific name: *Lucanus cervus*
Length: from about 0.3 in (8 mm) to 3.5 in (9 cm)
Key features: large, shiny body, large jaws, large **antennae**
Diet: sap that leaks from trees

Jaw

Thorax

Head

Antenna

Abdomen

Leg

UP CLOSE

Male stag beetles fight each other for females. They clash with their jaws, and try to push each other off a tree trunk.

Social Wasp

Social wasps often work as a team to build a large nest. Most of these wasps live together. Despite their name, not all social wasps are social. Some live alone.

Social wasps have a striped body and two pairs of wings. Only the females have a **stinger**. There are different kinds of social wasps. Paper wasps build their nest together. They make their nest by chewing up wood and weaving it. Each nest has a queen and many workers. Workers look after the young, catch **prey**, and guard the nest. The nest is filled with the flesh of their prey.

These social wasps are working together to build their nest.

FACT FILE

Common name: social wasps
Scientific name: Vespidae
Length: from about 0.2 in (5 mm) to 1.4 in (3.5 cm)
Key features: black and yellow or black-and-white striped body; females have a **stinger**
Diet: adults eat flower **nectar**, fruit, and tree **sap**; **larvae** eat **insects**

UP CLOSE

Some wasps cut up prey, such as a fly. This is so they can easily carry strips of it back to the nest.

Head

Antenna

Thorax

Waist

Fight to be Queen

Female wasps fight each other to become queen. Fights can last for several days. The queen is the only female allowed to lay eggs in the nest. Her eggs hatch into worker wasps. There may be 6,000 workers in a nest.

Leg

Abdomen

Wing

Flesh Fly

*Flesh flies are so called because their young feed upon the rotting flesh of dead and **decaying** animals.*

The female flesh fly lays her eggs inside rotting flesh. So when the **maggots** hatch out they have plenty to eat! They spit **digestive** juices on the food, which turns it into liquid. The maggots can eat liquid more easily than solid flesh.

Short antenna

Thorax

Head

Abdomen

Wing

Leg

FACT FILE

Common name: flesh fly
Scientific name: Sarcophagidae
Length: 0.08 in (2 mm) to 0.5 in (13 mm)
Key features: gray, striped **thorax**, red eyes, large feet, short **antennae**
Diet: adults eat flower **nectar**; maggots eat other **insects** and rotting flesh

Singer Parasite

Some female flesh flies are attracted by the singing of another bug, the male cicada. A female flesh fly flies to the cicada and lays her maggots inside his body. He makes a tasty meal for them!

Some flesh fly maggots steal food from the nests of wasps or bees. Their mother lays her eggs near the nest. When the maggots hatch they eat food in the nest that was meant for the young wasps or bees.

Flesh flies usually have large red eyes and a striped **thorax**.

Wolf Spider

It is not unusual to find these spiders in North American and European gardens. Wolf spiders are great hunters and one of the top killers of the bug world.

Wolf spiders do not catch their **prey** in a web. Instead, they pounce on prey. They have eight eyes. Two eyes are on top of their head, to the side. Two larger eyes are on the front of their head, and a row of four eyes are beneath. All these eyes help them spot their food. Wolf spiders eat **insects**. They inject their prey with poison before they eat it.

First row of eyes

Second row of eyes

The wolf spider's many eyes help it see in virtually every direction at the same time.

Hatching

Mother wolf spiders help their babies hatch from their eggs. The mother pulls off some of the tough egg coating so the baby can break out of the egg. Without this help the baby would die inside.

A wolf spider and its eggs.

Mouthpart

Head

Thorax

Leg

Abdomen

UP CLOSE

Males attract females by waving their front legs in the air. This sends a message to the female.

FACT FILE

Common name: wolf spider
Scientific name: *Lycosidae*
Length: from about 0.1 in (3 mm) to 1.4 in (3.5 cm)
Key features: three rows of eyes (the two largest eyes face forward), brown-black body
Diet: insects and other spiders

Cockroach

This pest is famous for running around people's kitchens! Luckily, most cockroaches run away from people. Only 25 of the 4,000 kinds of cockroach live among people.

Cockroaches eat almost anything. They especially like the waste food that people leave lying around. Cockroaches have a flattened body. This allows them to squeeze into small spaces, such as cracks in walls. Their front wings are tough and leathery. They also have long, thin **antennae**. Cockroaches generally come out to feed at night. They use their antennae to feel their way in the dark and to search for food.

This cockroach is feeding on a piece of bread.

UP CLOSE

Male cockroaches fight with each other over females. They try to push other males away. Males hiss loudly in battle, so fights can be very noisy!

Feeding Babies

Some cockroaches live in dead wood. The mother cockroach digs burrows in the wood, where she lays her eggs. When the eggs hatch, the mother feeds her babies on her milk.

Antenna

Head

Thorax

Abdomen

Leg

FACT FILE

Common name: cockroach
Scientific name: *Blattodea*
Length: from about 0.15 in (4 mm) to 4.8 in (12 cm)
Key features: flattened body, long antennae, leathery forewings
Diet: will eat almost anything

Ladybug

Everyone knows a ladybug when they see one! People love these spotty bugs, but they can be real pests, too.

Wing case

Antenna

Thorax

Abdomen

Leg

Hind wing

Head

Ladybugs are popular because they eat garden pests, such as **aphids**. But in some parts of the world these beetles are a real nuisance. There they eat the valuable crops, rather than protecting them from pests. Ladybugs are brightly colored, with black spots on a red or yellow body. Some ladybugs have lots of spots, others just a few. Their bright color warns **predators** to keep away. Ladybugs have short **antennae**, and you can hardly see their head at all.

Hungry Bugs

Big ladybugs eat about 25 aphids a day. If they run out of food, they may eat each other.

This ladybug is about to eat an aphid.

UP CLOSE

A male ladybug chooses its mate before she hatches! He chooses a **pupa** and sits on it until the female comes out. He fights off other males, then mates with the newly hatched female.

FACT FILE

Common name: ladybug
Scientific name: *Coccinellidae*
Length: from about 0.04 in (1 mm) to 0.4 in (10 mm)
Key features: bright red or yellow wing case with black spots, domed back, short antennae
Diet: aphids and other soft bugs; some ladybugs eat crops

Ladybugs spend most of the day on plants, looking for food.

Stink Bug

Stink bugs really do stink! They give off horrible smells so enemies, such as birds and lizards, keep well clear. If an animal does attack, it finds the bugs taste horrible.

Bug Snacks

Some stink bugs are meat eaters. They munch on ladybugs and moth **larvae**. They also eat other **prey** that are poisonous to birds or **mammals**, yet do not harm the stink bugs that eat them.

Adult stink bugs mostly feed on the juices, called **sap**, of smelly plants, such as cabbages. They store chemicals from the sap in glands on their **thorax** (chest). When a **predator** comes along, the bug lifts its **abdomen** and squirts the foul-smelling chemicals through holes on the underside of its body.

Antenna

Head

Wing

Leg

Thorax

Abdomen

FACT FILE

Common name: stink bug (shield bug)
Scientific name: Catacanthus anchorago
Length: from 0.2 in (4 mm) to 1 in (2.5 cm)
Key features: oval-shaped body with a rather flattened top; all adult stink bugs have wings
Diet: many feed on plant **sap**; others eat **insects**, especially ones with soft bodies, such as larvae (young)

Some stink bugs make "songs" to attract a mate. The bug scrapes a row of pegs on its leg against ridges on its tummy. It is a bit like playing a violin!

This stink bug's colorful body warns predators that it tastes foul. The bodies of other stink bugs are **camouflaged** to hide on plants.

23

Scarab Beetle

There are lots of different kinds of scarab beetles. Some come out to look for food at night, others by day. But they all have a favorite food in common, dung!

Scarab beetles have a thick, deep body and short, powerful legs. Some are brightly colored. Some male scarab beetles have amazing long horns. They use their horns to push each other over and off trees. Many scarabs feed on dung. They find dung by sensing it with their **antennae**. Then they roll it along the ground into a ball. They also lay their eggs in the dung. When the eggs hatch, the young scarab beetles eat the dung.

Female scarab beetles "ride" on top of a dung ball as the male beetle pushes it along. Females do this to protect the dung ball from other scarab beetles who might try to steal it!

Sacred Beetle

The ancient Egyptians worshiped scarab beetles. The Egyptians believed that their sun-god Re rolled the light across the sky each day, at dawn. The way that scarab beetles roll dung across the ground reminded them of their god.

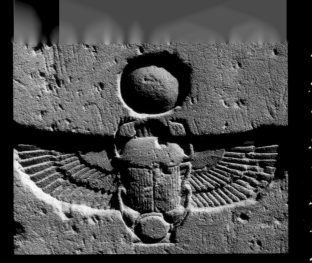

An ancient Egyptian carving of a scarab beetle.

UP CLOSE

Some scarab beetles are enormous. They can be heavier than birds! The male Hercules beetle weighs up to 2 oz (57 g) and can be 7 in (18 cm) long. Much of this length is its enormous front horn.

Large horn

Antenna

Thorax

Abdomen

Leg

FACT FILE

Common name: scarab beetle
Scientific name: *Scarabaeidae*
Length: from about 0.2 in (4 mm) to 7 in (18 cm)
Key features: round body, often brightly colored, large antennae
Diet: dung, leaves, roots, fruit, fungi, rotting meat; adults also eat **pollen** and **nectar**

Flea

*Fleas are the champion jumpers of the bug world. These **insects** can also carry diseases that are deadly to people, such as typhus.*

Fleas live on the bodies of **mammals** and birds. They eat their blood. A flea's flat shape helps it easily slip through the fur and feathers of its **host**. Fleas do not need wings, because they can jump so well. They leap from one animal to another. Fleas also drop their eggs around our homes. The **larvae** eat dead skin and crumbs left on floors and furniture. When the larvae hatch, they jump onto the nearest cat, dog, or person!

This photograph of a flea was taken by a powerful microscope. It shows the flea's very long mouthparts. The flea uses them to pierce its victim's skin and suck up its blood.

High Jump

Fleas have especially strong, muscular back legs. That allows them to jump 150 times farther than their body length and 80 times higher than their height.

Thorax

Leg

Head

Abdomen

Antenna

UP CLOSE

About 700 years ago, a terrible disease killed 75 million people. It was called bubonic plague, or the Black Death. The disease was carried by rats. Fleas bit the rats and caught the disease, too. They then bit people and passed the plague on.

FACT FILE

Common name: flea
Scientific name: *Siphonaptera*
Length: from about 0.04 in (1 mm) to 0.5 in (13 mm)
Key features: no wings, very flat body, legs adapted for jumping
Diet: adults feed only on blood; larvae feed on insects, faeces and vegetable matter.

Mantid

The mantid is an awesome bug killer, perfectly adapted for its deadly role. Mantids stand absolutely still as they wait for **prey**, then grab their victims as they pass.

Mantids are better known as praying mantises. They are so called because of the way they stand as they wait for their prey, with their front legs held forward. They look like they are praying! Mantids eat almost anything, including **insects**, spiders, and even small lizards. Their large eyes spot food easily, and their head can swivel in all directions to see. Mantids use their long, spiked legs to grip the prey. Then they munch through the unlucky bug.

Mantids can hold onto their prey with one front leg, and grab hold of another victim with the other.

Deadly Date

Sometimes a female mantid preys on the male while they are mating. She bites his head off! Luckily for the males this only seems to happen rarely, usually when the female is confused or very hungry.

Antenna

Head

Thorax

Front legs

Abdomen

Leg

UP CLOSE

The female mantid makes a special case from **foam** for her eggs. The case has lots of chambers, one for each egg. The hatched **nymphs** escape through a little hole at the top of each chamber.

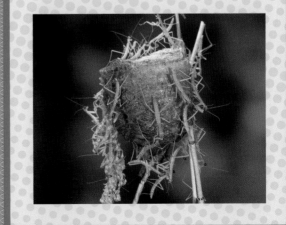

FACT FILE

Common name: praying mantid
Scientific name: *Mantodea*
Length: from about 0.4 in (10 mm) to 6 in (15 cm)
Key features: large eyes far apart, thin **antennae**, long **thorax**, leathery front wings
Diet: insects and spiders, sometimes lizards

Glossary

abdomen The rearmost part of an insect's body, behind the thorax.

antenna (antennae) A long, thin stalk on a bug's head, used for detecting movements, smells, and tastes.

aphid A tiny bug that sucks the juices from plants.

decaying Rotting.

digestive Breaking down food so it can be absorbed by the body.

foam A bubbling liquid, sometimes made by an animal.

host The animal upon which a parasite lives and feeds.

insect An animal with six legs and a body divided into three sections.

invertebrate An animal without a backbone (spine) or other bones.

larva (*pl.* larvae) The young stage in the life cycle of a bug, when it hatches out of its eggs.

maggot The young stage of a bug, when it has hatched but not yet become an adult.

mammal A warm-blooded animal that feeds its babies with milk and has fur or hair.

nectar A sugary liquid made by flowers to attract insects.

nymph A stage in the life cycle of some bugs; nymphs look like small adults without wings.

parasite An animal that lives on or in another animal.

pollen A yellow dust made by flowers so they can reproduce.

predator An animal that hunts other animals for food.

prey An animal that is hunted by another animal for food.

pupa A stage in the life cycle of some bugs, when they make hard covers round themselves. Inside the hard case, they turn into adults.

rostrum The mouthpart of a bedbug used to suck up blood.

sap A liquid made by plants or trees.

social Friendly.

stag A male deer.

stinger Part of an animal that can deliver a sting.

thorax The middle section of an insect's body, between the head and abdomen. The six legs are attached to the thorax.

Further Resources

Books about bugs

Do All Spiders Spin Webs?: Questions and Answers About Spiders by
  Melvin and Gilda Berger, Tandem Library, 2000

*Everything Bug: What Kids Really Want to Know About Insects and
  Spiders* by Cherie Winner, Northword, 2004

Life in a Bucket of Soil by Alvin and Virginia Silverstein, Dover
  Publications, 2000

The Best Book of Bugs by Claire Llewellyn, Kingfisher, 2005

Useful websites

http://earthlife.net/insects/six.html

www.ivyhall.district96.k12.il.us/4TH/KKHP/1insects/bugmenu.html

http://www5.pbrc.hawaii.edu/microangela/

Index